# THE DARK
## OF THE

# DARK
## SUN

SELECTED
POEMS OF
UMBERTO
S A B A
TRANSLATED BY
CHRISTOPHER
M I L L I S

UNIVERSITY
PRESS OF
AMERICA

Lanham • New York • London

Copyright © 1994 by
**University Press of America® Inc.**
4720 Boston Way
Lanham, Maryland 20706

3 Henrietta Street
London WC2E 8LU England

Book design, typography & electronic pagination
by Arrow Graphics, Inc.
Watertown, Massachusetts

**Library of Congress Cataloging-in-Publication Data**

Saba, Umberto, 1883–1957.
[Canzoniere. English & Italian. Selections]
The dark of the sun : selected poems of Umberto Saba /
Translated by Christopher Millis.
p.      cm.
Poems in Italian with English translation on opposite pages.
Poems selected chiefly from Il canzoniere (1961) and a few
selected from Tutte le poesie (1988).
1. Saba, Umberto, 1883–1957—Translations into English.
I. Millis, Christopher.   II. Title.
PQ4841.A18A25      1993      851'.912—dc20      93–35508 CIP

ISBN 0–8191–9330–5 (cloth : alk. paper)

Cover design by Aramais Andonian

 The paper used in this publication meets the minimum requirements of
American National Standard for Information Sciences—Permanence
of Paper for Printed Library Materials, ANSI Z39.48–1984.

# ACKNOWLEDGMENTS

| | |
|---|---|
| *Anthology of Magazine Verse & Yearbook of American Poetry* | Woman |
| *Colorado Review* | Winter |
| *International Poetry Review* | Produce, Woman, The Goat |
| *Missouri Review* | Insomnia on a Summer Night, Sapling, Trieste |
| *New Letters* | House of My Babysitter, Warning |
| *Paintbrush* | In the Courtyard, Happiness |
| *Seneca Review* | To My Wife, After a Walk, Letter to a Friend... |

Special thanks to the Commission for Educational and Cultural Exchange for the Fulbright Grant which permitted completion of this project.

For the generous attention of Mitchell Leaska, Ruth Castalde, Antonio Corsaro, Deborah Lyons, Deborah Tall, Jeffrey Skinner, David Weiss, Sarah Gorham, Elena Botteri, Nora Baldi, Lionello Zorn, Rafaella Giorni, and for the Yaddo Corporation's providing me luxurious solitude, I am grateful.

"Amore," "Ulisse," "Il poeta e il conformista," "L'uomo e gli animali," "Al lettore," and "Epigrafe" are from *Tutte Le Poesie* by Umberto Saba (copyright 1988) and appear courtesy of Arnoldo Mondadori Editore, Milano. The remaining poems are from *Il Canzoniere* by Umberto Saba (copyright 1961) and appear courtesy of Giulio Einaudi Editore, Torino.

For you, Nina.

# TABLE OF CONTENTS

Foreword                                    vii

Introduction                                  1

I.  Poems 1909 – 1934

    The Goat                                  7

    A Memory                                  9

    To My Wife                               11

    The Beautiful Thought                    17

    "Produce"                                19

    Guido                                    21

    Picture of My Daughter                   25

    The Farewell                             27

    After a Walk                             29

    The Poet                                 31

    Trieste                                  33

    Sapling                                  35

    The Pier                                 37

    Woman                                    39

    Three Streets                            41

    The Kid with the Wheelbarrow             45

    Insomnia on a Summer Night               47

    The Song of One Morning                  49

    After Sadness                            53

    Border Town                              55

    Three Cities

        1. Milan                             57

        2. Turin                             59

        3. Florence                          61

    The Cat                                  63

    Winter                                   65

    Finale                                   67

## II.  Poems 1900 – 1908

Glauco                                    71
The House of My Babysitter                73
For Mother                                75
In the Courtyard                          83
Letter to a Friend Studying
Piano at the Conservatory of...           85
Warning                                   91

## III.  Poems 1935 – 1953

Broken Glass                              95
Love                                      97
Ulysses                                   99
The Poet and the Conformist              101
Man and Animals                          103
Happiness                                105
To the Reader                            107
Ashes                                    109
Words                                    111
Epigraph                                 113

# FOREWORD

For a late twentieth-century reader, the immediacy and apparent simplicity of Umberto Saba's poetry open one door while shutting another. These qualities, so prevalent in contemporary poetry (perhaps especially in American poetry), make his writing almost too easy to read. It is so accessible that the nature of his achievement is obscured. We miss the shock, the scandal, of these verses for the early twentieth-century Italian reader.

A second distinctive characteristic of Saba's work, which is apparent in the translator's careful selection, is the creation and re-creation of a single collection. From 1921 on, Saba began to organize his poetry under the title — with all its Petrarchan resonances — of *Canzoniere*. By choosing a structure that strictly respects actual chronology, he attempted to give his collection the character of a journey, a history, an existential biography, even a novel, with all the psychological, as well as narrative, implications that term carries in the twentieth century. This structure becomes a key for reading, inviting us to take the experience as a whole, an ensemble in which the "impure" parts, the "ballast" — as Saba liked to say, the shadow-zones of inspiration, play an essential role alongside the most inspired moments.

This construction of a poetic "biography" from the materials of daily life clearly harmonizes with the everyday quality of this verse. Throughout a poetic career of more than fifty years, Saba pursued and perfected this mainstay of his poetics, making it a fixed point of reference. This was clearly a risky proposition, one that placed Saba in opposition to the prevailing trend towards a formally and thematically complex poetry. This choice of his provoked misunderstanding and perplexity, since the modest everyday appearance of his poems was sometimes taken for the obviousness and facility typical of "minor" poetry. But in the end, the approach won out, as is clear from the position Saba now occupies in the history of Italian poetry. This recognition is largely due to his dedication to that ideal of *clarity* which Saba understood to be the poet's unique and unrenounceable ability.

It has never been easy for those who love Saba to describe the character of his poetic writings with adequate rigor. Something always seems to escape the attention of the reader, who remains dazzled by an immediate perception of beauty and profundity. For Saba, existence was varied — ample, abundant, and disjoint, extending in all directions, dominated by habit, but also by aesthetic impurity. It could be said that for Saba, the surface of experience, its form, perceptible and taken for granted as it is, necessarily coincides with its final meanings. This does not reduce experience to the mere worship of *things* gradually convertible into *words*, which would force poetry to bear a more purely metaphoric or symbolic burden. To take what one finds in the world, in all its ordinariness — stories, interior lives, portraits, characters, and turn it into an object of beauty without stripping it of meaning — this is the poet's task. It is only by respecting its intimate contours that poetry can transform ordinary experience into an extraordinary act.

For the rest, no words could better express the poet's alchemy of the ordinary than those of Saba himself. "The poet has his allotted time,/ like everybody else,/ but what variety! . . . He returns flushed at sunset,/ and with the onset of clouds/ his happiness changes,/ if not his heart." (*The Poet*).

The relationship between sadness and desire is everywhere in Saba's poetry. But it is also a relationship which the verse proposes to resolve harmoniously, at times almost before it is expressed. A key to this, as well as other aspects of his poetry, is the geo-cultural area in which Saba lived and worked. In the early years of this century, Trieste, once a border-town, completely marginalized in its distance from the centers of artistic activity, became in its turn a center from which the latest culture emanated. This was a culture which found in sadness and anguish, for the first time, the projections of an interior psychic conflict. Saba's "geographic" modernity must always be kept in mind, for it is the source of a conscious-ness, innate to his work, of the inevitable weight — whether biological or historical — of the pressure of death. Indeed this schism, this historic wound, is brought to the surface, at once nullified and implied in the continued insistence on its opposite, which could perhaps be identified with the Freudian plea-sure principle.

Clearly, however, the language of psychoanalysis leaves no mark on the poetry. It can only be glimpsed from within a framework which has remained faithful to the traditional discourse of the sentiments. In the early Saba, everything seems to hinge on simple con-trasts of images and situations, as for instance in *Glauco*, a poem of almost schematic architecture. Here melancholy and the lightness of being are placed side-by-side in the most candid of childhood memories. "What's the thought/ you won't say that removes you? You can't imagine how wonderful life feels/ for the friends you run off from,/ how the time soars, alive and fantastic." Here what wins out is the "unsaid", that element of "biological" melancholy which the reader perceives lurking behind the repression. But elsewhere, melancholy cannot be resolved simply by a trick of the light. Instead, anguish and torment, tightly bound up with beauty, become themselves sources of beauty. "And who could have said my life would/ be so wonderful, such sweet sorrow/ and such secluded bliss!" *(After Sadness)*. Here, even more obviously, the repression is all in the choice of words, as the meaning of "sorrow" is channeled into one of the oldest and most familiar phrases, "sweet sorrows."

With this example, we come to a defining aspect of Saba's poetic experience, the idea of a poetics capable above all of dissolving unsatisfied desire, that desire which occurs in every life, but which also forces a constriction and withholding of life. Poetry should be able to recall this desire, but through a process of distillation or illumination, and most of all, of *reason*. "Life is grim and full of grief,/ and nothing about it is certain...For thinking these things/ one takes a hit to the middle/ of the heart. Art helps keep me/ from such thoughts; it turns the fragments/ of a life into something singular and beautiful. One good line/ restores me." This is the mature Saba, now in complete control of a poetry that synthesizes and totalizes his experience.

Saba, as we have said, was far-removed from any poetry or poetics of his time. No tortured expression of psychic anguish and disintegration, his verse becomes the instrument of a higher exorcism, recomposing sadness into clarity, lightness, and tranquillity.

His verse is far from any aestheticizing tradition which looks to poetry for beauty not found in life; and it is just as far from the Crocean idea of poetry as some absolute and unrepeatable lyric moment. But it is likewise removed from the prevailing twentieth-century Italian tradition, which makes of poetry a sophisticated intellectual tool, formally and stylistically daring. If Saba's eye is naked, without binoculars or microscope, his language is also poor in imagination, resistant to experiment, forcedly obedient to formal pronouncements and the most canonical and established meters. Paradoxical as it might seem, there is an absolute modernity in this strange alchemy which can insert ordinary, everyday language into metrical and syntactic contexts that are wholly literary.

For Saba, the rigor of meter is what holds poetry together, and allows the poetic utterance to come into contact with the eternal simulacrum. If in the poetry of the twentieth century, traditional meters are a technical point of departure or, in some cases, an ideal but far-off goal, something which precedes or follows the concrete organization of the verse, for Saba these are the immanence of the poem, the limit, the cage which encloses inspiration.

In the same way, archaism, literary language, syntax and diction redolent of scholasticism, all have their rightful place in the humble modernity of the poet's preferred themes and situations. They unite with everyday language, and the effect is never strident or forced. Rather, they mingle without artificiality or conceit, but with a naturalness and spontaneity that thrives on fusion and fluidity. In this union of the literary and the everyday, Saba has deliberately chosen a language that is more than usually dense, but without drama. By attending carefully to Saba's quotidian elegance, which shines through in the translations of Christopher Millis, we can begin to appreci-

ate one of the most unusual developments in twenti-
eth–century poetry, a verse that is wholly and com-
pletely foreign, stateless in its freedom from all con-
vention.

Antonio Corsaro

Translated by Deborah Lyons

# INTRODUCTION

By rights Umberto Saba should never have been a poet. He was poor, quit school at age sixteen, was born into an Italian city where German was spoken — Trieste of the late Austro-Hungarian Empire — and lived in a home where there were no books. By rights, he should have been a salesman.

In fact, he was. Saba's marginality, a rural, a Jew in Italy of the nineteen thirties and forties, and eventually a fussy bookstore proprietor, made him become what we normally think of as exclusively postmodern: the artist as self-publicist. Saba waged a life-long war for acceptance against the literary mainstream of his day. One of the more interesting battles included a book-length analysis of his then recently published Collected Poems which Saba wrote himself under a pseudonym.

Saba's literary battles complemented his personal ones. Italian fascism weighed heavily on a poor Italian Jew coming from the only city in Italy to build a concentration camp. In *Scorciatoie e raccontini* where Saba writes about the war, one hears a curious quality in his voice, an ironic detachment nearly, and a sense of the war as not so terribly strange. After all, the fascists were only one of the forces out to annihilate him.

Saba said about himself that he knew he would not be a success. How he said it is telling: "Io so di essere votato all' insucesso." He did not say judged and he did not say considered, literally he said he knew he would be voted unsuccessful. *Votato* suggests in both cultures the suspicious movement of politics and hints at Saba's larger sights. His life-long clamoring for public attention was exactly proportional to his contempt for it; he wanted badly what he knew did not matter. In that respect he was a deeply self-destructive man. One hears that as a gregarious remorse in his poetry; the human objects of Saba's attention seldom merit it, and the poet knows.

The inner circle of Saba's personal life was, like his months of hiding in Florence before the war's end, unobtrusively chaotic. While Saba himself and many of his critics would have us believe him a retiring provincial, he was not. Nora Baldi, an intimate friend of Saba's late in his life, put it this way: "He loved everybody. He loved the girls and he loved the boys; he loved women and he loved men." He also loved his wife, to whom he was married for 46 years until her death a year before his own. Helpless before his need to defy, Saba read the Our Father at her burial in the Jewish cemetery of Trieste.

When Umberto Saba died in 1957 alone in a hospital in Europe's other divided city, Gorizia, just north of Trieste, the vote on his career was already changing. The shape the change took would have pleased Saba, since it was not the academic community but other writers who conferred on him the praise he insisted he deserved. Pasolini, Montale and Morante, among others, as well as one noteworthy critic, Giacomo Debenedetti, who recognized Saba's importance early on, were in the avant-garde of his admirers. The critical world has since followed suit.

On the other hand, Saba's detractors were not entirely wrong. He was, early in his career, altogether too attached to archaisms which gave his verse a stilted quality. And his championing of his own personality and daily life in his work does make the reader wish at times for a formal narrative distance. His critics were not wrong so much as shortsighted; he outgrew his nineteenth century diction and his *biografis-mo* is the source of some of the most intoxicating, poignant lyricism our century has seen.

Translating Saba's poetry into English is like turning a kiss into a handshake. The cultural differences are subtle and extreme: where the Italian is demonstrative and intimate, for the English to work it must be comparatively understated and public. If the nuance and depth of the sentiment are to cross cultures and time, then the Italian cannot be snubbed and the English cannot be shocked. For every three mentions of "Mama," for instance, in the original, I have repeated it once in translation, and not as mama but as mother.

The poems in this volume represent an introduction to Saba. A fraction of his complete work, their arrangement is also introductory. Beginning with the verse of his maturity, the sequence moves backwards to his youth and forward again to a selection from his final volumes. Saba's is a poetry of suffering and celebration, sensuality and defeat. As an early installment of his work in English, these translations are intended as a lingering handshake, the sort that may become a kiss.

Christopher Millis
Geneva, New York

Poems 1909 – 1934

## La capra

Ho parlato a una capra.
Era sola sul prato, era legata.
Sazia d'erba, bagnata
dalla pioggia, belava.

Quell'uguale belato era fraterno
al mio dolore. Ed io risposi, prima
per celia, poi perché il dolore è eterno,
ha una voce e non varia.
Questa voce sentiva
gemere in una capra solitaria.

In una capra dal viso semita
sentiva querelarsi ogni altro male,
ogni altra vita.

## The Goat

I have spoken to a goat.
She was alone in a field, she was leashed.

Glutted with grass, soaked
from rain, she bleated.
That level bleat brothered
my pain. And I responded, first
to fool, then, since sadness hears its name,
I spoke the same staccato.
The throat knows
the anguish of a single goat.

In a goat's semitic snout
I heard the cry of every trouble
of every living thing.

## Un ricordo

Non dormo. Vedo una strada, un boschetto,
che sul mio cuore come un'ansia preme;
dove si andava, per star soli e insieme,
io e un altro ragazzetto.

Era la Pasqua; i riti lunghi e strani
dei vecchi. E se non mi volesse bene
— pensavo — e non venisse più domani?
E domani non venne. Fu un dolore,
uno spasimo fu verso la sera;
che un'amicizia (oggi lo so) non era,
era quello un amore;

il primo; e quale e che felicità
n'ebbi, tra i colli e il mare di Trieste.
Ma perché non dormire, oggi, con queste
storie di, credo, quindici anni fa?

## A Memory

I can't sleep. I'm watching a street and a park
that nearly hurt me to look at;
we used to go there, to be alone and together,
another boy and me.

It was Easter; the old people
did their strange, elaborate things. What if —
I thought — he doesn't like me and tomorrow he
                              doesn't show up?
Tomorrow he did not show up. Then there was pain,
a kind of spasm toward night;
(today I know) that was no friendship,
that was love;

the first, and there was joy in it
between the hills and the sea of Trieste.
But why can't I sleep, today,
when this happened, I think, fifteen years ago?

## A mia moglie

Tu sei come una giovane,
una bianca pollastra.
Le si arruffano al vento
le piume, il collo china
per bere, e in terre raspa;
ma, nell'andare, ha il lento
tuo passo di regina,
ed incede sull'erba
pettoruta e superba.
È migliore del maschio.
È come sono tutte
le femmine di tutti
i sereni animali
che avvicinano a Dio.
Cosí se l'occhio, se il giudizio mio
non m'inganna, fra queste hai le tue uguali,
e in nessun'altra donna.
Quando la sera assonna
le gallinelle,
mettono voci che ricordan quelle,
dolcissime, onde a volte dei tuoi mali
ti quereli, e non sai
che la tua voce ha la soave e triste
musica dei pollai.

Tu sei come una gravida
giovenca;
libera ancora e senza
gravezza, anzi festosa;
che, se la lisci, il collo
volge, ove tinge un rosa
tenero la sua carne.

## To My Wife

You're like a young lady,
a young lady hen.
In the wind she ruffles
her feathers, neck poised
to drink, and scratches the ground;
but in moving she wears the slow
progress of queens,
and strides over grass
strutting and superb.
She humbles the male.
And she's one
with all females
of all the untroubled creatures
who come close to God.
If my mind and my eyes
don't deceive me, you have your equal
in them and in no other woman.
When the night puts the chickens
to sleep, they sound
like when you mutter to yourself,
but sweetly, and you're not aware
how your own voice has the tender, sad
music of hens.

You're like a pregnant
heifer,
still spry and unweighty,
even willing to play;
if you pet her,
she'll rotate her neck
till it reddens.

Se l'incontri e muggire
l'odi, tanto è quel suono
lamentoso, che l'erba
strappi, per farle un dono.
È cosí che il mio dono
t'offro quando sei triste.

Tu sei come una lunga
cagna, che sempre tanta
dolcezza ha negli occhi,
e ferocia nel cuore.
Ai tuoi piedi una santa
sembra, che d'un fervore
indomabile arda,
e cosí ti riguarda
come il suo Dio e Signore.
Quando in casa o per via
segue, a chi solo tenti
avvicinarsi, i denti
candidissimi scopre.
Ed il suo amore soffre
di gelosia.

Tu sei come la pavida
coniglia. Entro l'angusta
gabbia ritta al vederti
s'alza,
e verso di te gli orecchi
alti protende e fermi;
che la crusca e i radicchi
tu le porti, di cui
priva in sé si rannicchia,
cerca gli angoli bui.
Chi potrebbe quel cibo
ritoglierle? chi il pelo

If you meet her she'll low,
but if it upsets you,
if the sound seems too sad,
make her a gift
of a wad of grass.
In the same spirit
I give you gifts when you're sad.

You're like your own
faithful dog,
with kind eyes
and a snarling heart.
At your feet, it's a panting
fanatic who looks up to you,
master and God.
She trails you at home
and out in the street,
so if you get close to anyone
her lip lifts over her teeth.
And her love suffers
from a rivalrous hate.

You're like a scared
rabbit. She springs up when she sees you
from her narrow cage, then tracks you
with those tall, immobile ears;
you bring her scraps
when she's hungry, and she crouches,
darting for dark corners.
Who could take food from her?

che si strappa di dosso,
per aggiungerlo al nido
dove poi partorire?
Chi mai farti soffrire?

Tu sei come la rondine
che torna in primavera.
Ma in autunno riparte;
e tu non hai quest'arte.
Tu questo hai della rondine:
le movenze leggere;
questo che a me, che mi sentiva ed era
vecchio, annunciavi un'altra primavera.

Tu sei come la provvida
formica. Di lei, quando
escono alla campagna,
parla al bimbo la nonna
che l'accompagna.
E cosí nella pecchia
ti ritrovo, ed in tutte
le femmine di tutti
i sereni animali
che avvicinano a Dio;
e in nessun'altra donna.

Who could skin the pelt she pulls at
to make a nest for her litter?
Who could ever hurt you?

You're like the swallow that returns every spring.
But the swallow goes away every autumn;
you fail at this art.
But you have this of the swallow;
the light movements
that used to make me feel
old, when you'd signal yet another spring.

You're like the well-prepared
ant whom grandmothers
point out to children
on their walks in the country.
And so I see you in the bee
and in all females
of all the untroubled creatures
who come close to God
and in no other woman.

## Il bel pensiero

Avevo un bel pensiero e l'ho perduto.
Uno di quei pensieri che tra il sonno
e la veglia consolano la casta
adolescenza; e ben di rado poi
fan ritorno fra noi.

Io perseguivo il mio pensiero come
si persegue una bella creatura,
che ne conduce ove a lei piace, ed ecco:
perdi per sempre la sua leggiadria
a una svolta di via.

Una voce profana, un importuno
richiamo il bel pensiero in fuga han messo.
Ora lo cerco in ciechi labirinti
d'inferno, e so ch'esser non può lontano,
ma che sperarlo è vano.

## The Beautiful Thought

I had a beautiful thought and I lost it.
One of those thoughts between waking
and sleep that can console
an adolescent; the kind we rarely have
for one another any more.

I pursued my thought
like one pursues a beautiful creature
that goes wherever it pleases, and there it was:
that loveliness lost forever
at a turn in the road.

I cursed, I demanded
my beautiful thought come back.
Now I look for it in the blind alleys
of hell, and I know it's not far,
but hoping is useless.

## «Frutta erbaggi»

Erbe, frutta, colori della bella
stagione. Poche ceste ove alla sete
si rivelano dolci polpe crude.

Entra un fanciullo colle gambe nude,
imperioso, fugge via.
                        S'oscura
l'umile botteguccia, invecchia come
una madre.
            Di fuori egli nel sole
si allontana, con l'ombra sua, leggero.

**"Produce"**


Greens, fruits, colors of the sweet
season. Baskets brag at their brims
of ripe fibers.

Enter a boy with bare legs,
imperious, who passes quickly.

    Night
mutes the market like a dark mother.

    Outside in the sun
he steps with his shadow, lightly.

## Guido

Sul campo, ove a frugar tra l'erba siede,
mi scorge, e in fretta a sé mi chiama, o impronto
s'appressa, come chi un compagno vede;

sciocchissimo fanciullo, a cui colora
le guance un rosa di nubi al tramonto,
e ai quindici anni non par giunto ancora.

Parla di nevicate e di radicchi,
e del paese ove ha uno zio bifolco.
Poi, senza ch'altri lo rincorra o picchi,

fugge da me che intento l'ho ascoltato;
or lo guardo tenersi bene al solco,
non mai, correndo, entrar nel seminato.

Giunto al cancello, lo vedrò in quel tratto
tornarmi, se non fa il verso al tacchino,
o non mi scorda per l'amor che ratto

nasce tra un cane giovane e un bambino.

Ma spesso, per dovere o per trastullo,
come un buon padre o un amoroso balio,
conduce a mano un piccolo fanciullo.

E in giorno di lavoro né s'aggira
pei campi, né alla scuola è il suo travaglio.
La mamma sua fuor del caldo lo tira,

assonnato lo manda all'officina;
non vede come ai giovanetti è bello
di primavera dormir la mattina.

# Guido

He makes me out at a distance
where he's busy scrounging the ground, and shouts
or rushes up to me, as if we were long-lost friends;

a blockheaded boy, whose cheeks
color like clouds in a sunset
and at fifteen still seem as smooth.

He talks about snowfalls and lettuce
and the village where his uncle's a farmer.
Then, as if battered by furies,

he flies off, convinced that I've listened.
I follow his high wire act where a plow's been,
he runs and never falls in.

At his gate I'll watch him
turn again my way, unless there's a poem
to recite to his turkeys, or he forgets me

for the love of a dog and a boy.

Often, either obliged or for fun,
like a good father or a loving nurse,
he walks a small child by the hand.

But Monday to Friday he wanders no field,
nor suffers out hours at school.
His mother hauls him from where it's warm

and packs him off sleepy to work.
She forgets the pleasure it is to be young
and sleep late in the morning in spring.

Là un po' s'annoia, un po' ride schiamazza;
che il mastro, o un piú di lui grosso monello
lo insegue in una lunga corsa pazza.

Chi lo giunge lo mette rovescioni,
e se lo serra fra i duri ginocchi.
Ride il vinto, trattato a sculaccioni,

e ridendo si sente punger gli occhi.

Guido ha qualcosa dell'anima mia,
dell'anima di tante creature;
e tiene in cuore la sua nostalgia.

Gli dico: «Non verrai con me a Trieste?
Là c'è il mestiere per tutti, e c'è pure
da divertirsi domeniche e feste».

«Laggiú dove ci son — dice — gli slavi?»
«Vedessi — dico — la bella montagna,
e il mar dove d'aprile già ti lavi.»

«E a Tripoli — risponde — c'è mai stato?»;
e si piega a frugar tra l'erbaspagna,
e a mostrarmi un radicchio che ha strappato.

«Vedessi i nuovi bastimenti, il molo
di sera»...e vedo irradiarsi in volto
Guido, che vuol andare, oh sí, ma solo

a Casalecchio, ove ha uno zio bifolco.

There he gets bored till he's noisy
when his boss or some other ox in the office
chases him around.

The one who grabs him cuffs his ears
then locks him in a vise of knees.
The victim laughs at being spanked

so hard it stings his eyes.

Guido's soul is partly mine
and partly every creature's;
he keeps his feelings to himself.

I say to him, "Why not come with me to Trieste?
There's work for everybody
and you'd even have weekends free."

"Down there," he says, "where Slovenians live?"
"You'd see," I tell him, "beautiful mountains,
and in April you can swim in the sea."

"Have you been to Tripoli?" he wants to know,
and bending down among the weeds
pulls up a lettuce to show me.

"You'd see the new ships, and the pier
when the sun sets"...I see his face light up,
yes, Guido wants to go

as far as Casalecchio, where his uncle's a farmer.

## Ritratto della mia bambina

La mia bambina con la palla in mano,
con gli occhi grandi colore del cielo
e dell'estiva vesticciola: «Babbo
— mi disse — voglio uscire oggi con te».
Ed io pensavo: Di tante parvenze
che s'ammirano al mondo, io ben so a quali
posso la mia bambina assomigliare.
Certo alla schiuma, alla marina schiuma
che sull'onde biancheggia, a quella scia
ch'esce azzurra dai tetti e il vento sperde;
anche alle nubi, insensibili nubi
che si fanno e disfanno in chiaro cielo;
e ad altre cose leggere e vaganti.

## Picture of My Daughter

My daughter with a ball in hand,
with her big, sky-colored eyes
and a summer dress, said to me, "Daddy,
today I want us to go out."
I used to think: Of all the shapes
one admires in the world, I know
which ones my daughter resembles.
Certainly foam, the sea foam
that whitens waves, and the wakes
that drift blue from roofs in the wind;
and clouds, the insensitive clouds
that form and unform in a clear sky;
and other things errant and slight.

## L'addio

Senz'addii m'hai lasciato e senza pianti;
    devo di ciò accorarmi?
Tu non piangevi perché avevi tanti
    tanti baci da darmi.

Durano sí certe amorose intese
    quanto una vita e piú.
Io so un amore che ha durato un mese,
    e vero amore fu.

## The Farewell

Without so much as a word you left me,
     let alone a tear.
But you used to have so many kisses to give
     what should I fear?

Some lovers last a lifetime together
     and still they're not through.
I know a love that lasted a month,
     and it was love, too.

## Dopo una passeggiata

Quando fino ad un colle o lungo il mare
noi pure usciamo nelle belle sere
a passeggiare,
vedo che a tutti appare
cosa fraterna l'alleanza nostra.
Noi cui la vita tanto sangue costa
e tanta inusitata gioia rende,
nulla abbiamo che in vista il volgo offende;
siamo a tutti due buoni, due tranquilli
cittadini, a cui mèta è un buon bicchiere.
Solo nei cuori rispondono squilli,
si spiegano al vento bandiere.

E nei giorni di festa, se pur tanto
v'ha di strano, che cerco il piú deserto
dei sobborghi, chi mai vedrebbe in noi
altro che due che cenano all'aperto?
Un marito che già ostenta un rimpianto
di libertà, una moglie gelosa;
non v'ha, dico, una cosa
che dai molti distingua, amica, noi,

noi che rechiamo in cuore
i nostri due avversi destini
d'arte e d'amore.

## After a Walk

We still go out when the weather's warm
at night along the hills or sea
and I watch how others look at us
like walking proof of harmony.
We who've paid a price in blood
and grew older while its pleasures thinned,
do nothing that might raise an eye;
we are the calm respectable
types, two contented passers-by.
Though something in us rises up
to hear the flags beat in the wind.

And holidays, who'd ever think
to roam the most deserted street
meant more than being on a search
for someplace out of doors to eat?
A husband failing
at his guilt, a jealous wife,
do not, I say, make us distinct,
instead, friend,

they call to heart
our warring fates
of love and art.

## Il poeta

Il poeta ha le sue giornate
contate,
come tutti gli uomini; ma quanto,
quanto variate!

L'ore del giorno e le quattro stagioni,
un po' meno di sole o piú di vento,
sono lo svago e l'accompagnamento
sempre diverso per le sue passioni
sempre le stesse; ed il tempo che fa
quando si leva, è il grande avvenimento
del giorno, la sua gioia appena desto.
Sovra ogni aspetto lo rallegra questo
d'avverse luci, le belle giornate
movimentate
come la folla in una lunga istoria,
dove azzurro e tempesta poco dura,
e si alternano messi di sventura
e di vittoria.
Con un rosso di sera fa ritorno,
e con le nubi cangia di colore
la sua felicità,
se non cangia il suo cuore.

Il poeta ha le sue giornate
contate,
come tutti gli uomini; ma quanto,
quanto beate!

## The Poet

The poet has his allotted time
like everybody else,
but what variety!

Twenty-four hours a day, four seasons,
a little sun or a little wind,
these are his flings and his steady companion
always new to his senses
always the same; the big event
of the day is the weather
when he gets up, the excitement rises.
He thrills at changes
in light, how days
proceed like history,
blue skies and storms,
bad luck and victory.
He returns flushed at sunset,
and with an onset of clouds
his happiness changes,
if not his heart.

The poet has his allotted time
like everybody else,
but what bliss!

# Trieste

Ho attraversata tutta la città.
Poi ho salita un'erta,
popolosa in principio, in là deserta,
chiusa da un muricciolo:
un cantuccio in cui solo
siedo; e mi pare che dove esso termina
termini la città.

Trieste ha una scontrosa
grazia. Se piace,
è come un ragazzaccio aspro e vorace,
con gli occhi azzurri e mani troppo grandi
per regalare un fiore;
come un amore
con gelosia.
Da quest'erta ogni chiesa, ogni sua via
scopro, se mena all'ingombrata spiaggia,
o alla collina cui, sulla sassosa
cima, una casa, l'ultima, s'aggrappa.
Intorno
circola ad ogni cosa
un'aria strana, un'aria tormentosa,
l'aria natia.

La mia città che in ogni parte è viva,
ha il cantuccio a me fatto, alla mia vita
pensosa e schiva.

# Trieste

I've walked the entire city.
Then I've climbed a hill
dense at first, but empty further on,
closed in by a low stone wall:
I sit alone in one of its nooks
and it seems to me that where it ends
the city ends as well.

Trieste has an irritating
grace. At best,
it's like some mean, delinquent kid
with blue eyes and hands too big
to give anyone a flower;
it's like love
jealousy infects.
From the hill I can see
all the churches, and every street
that leads to the obstructed beach,
or across to another hill
where the last house clings
to the stony top.
Everywhere the air moves
it feels strangely troubled
like the air of being home.

My city that's alive in all its parts
has a place for me,
for my removed, reflective life.

## L'arboscello

Oggi il tempo è di pioggia.
Sembra il giorno una sera,
sembra la primavera
un autunno, ed un gran vento devasta
l'arboscello che sta — e non pare — saldo;
par tra le piante un giovanetto alto
troppo per la sua troppo verde età.
Tu lo guardi. Hai pietà
forse di tutti quei candidi fiori
che la bora gli toglie; e sono frutta,
sono dolci conserve
per l'inverno quei fiori che tra l'erbe
cadono. E se ne duole la tua vasta
maternità.

## Sapling

Today it's raining.
Day seems like night,
spring seems like autumn,
and a strong wind wastes a sapling
which doesn't seem solid.
It looks like a boy among plants,
lanky and light colored.
When you see him pity fills you
for blossoms beheaded by the gales;
fruit and their sweet winter jams
die where flowers touch grass.
Your grief is as vast as maternity.

## Il molo

Per me al mondo non v'ha un piú caro e fido
luogo di questo. Dove mai piú solo
mi sento e in buona compagnia che al molo
San Carlo, e piú mi piace l'onda e il lido?

Vedo navi il cui nome è già un ricordo
d'infanzia. Come allor torbidi e fiacchi
— forse aspettando dell'imbarco l'ora —
i garzoni s'aggirano; quei sacchi
su quella tolda, quelle casse a bordo
di quel veliero, eran principio un giorno
di gran ricchezze, onde stupita avrei
l'accolta folla a un lieto mio ritorno,
di bei doni donati i fidi miei.
Non per tale un ritorno or lascerei
molo San Carlo, quest'estrema sponda
d'Italia, ove la vita è ancora guerra;
non so, fuori di lei, pensar gioconda
l'opera, i giorni miei quasi felici,
cosí ben profondate ho le radici
nella mia terra.

Né a te dispiaccia, amica mia, se amore
reco pur tanto al luogo ove son nato.
Sai che un piú vario, un piú movimentato
porto di questo è solo il nostro cuore.

## The Pier

There is no place in the world I love better
than this. Where else can I feel more alone, where else
am I never abandoned, than the pier at San Carlo,
and where's there a better surf or beach?

I see the ships whose names I knew
as a child. And the same slack, troubled
dockboys listing about, waiting for the hour
they'll set sail; these bags
on that deck; those trunks aboard there,
those were the days
I saw dizzying wealth, and crowds gathered
awestruck at my casual return
to lay such homage before me.
Not even for that reception
would I leave San Carlo now,
the pier where Italy ends, the place where life
is still war; away from there, I can't imagine
how work could be fun
or my days could be half as happy,
so fixed am I
in that ground.

My friend, don't let it upset you
if I love the place I was born so much.
You know the heart's harbor
is more excitable still.

## Donna

Quand'eri
giovinetta pungevi
come una mora di macchia. Anche il piede
t'era un'arma, o selvaggia.

Eri difficile a prendere.
                    Ancora
giovane, ancora
sei bella. I segni
degli anni, quelli del dolore, legano
l'anime nostre, una ne fanno. E dietro
i capelli nerissimi che avvolgo
alle mie dita, piú non temo il piccolo
bianco puntuto orecchio demoniaco.

## Woman

When you were
a girl you pricked
like a blackberry. Even your foot
was a weapon, oh wild one.

You were hard to take.
                         Now
woman, still
you are beautiful. Tangles
of years of hurting tie up
our souls into one. Behind
the darkest hair that I wind
in my fingers, I'm no longer afraid
of the little white pointed demon ear.

## Tre vie

C'è a Trieste una via dove mi specchio
nei lunghi giorni di chiusa tristezza:
si chiama Via del Lazzaretto Vecchio.
Tra case come ospizi antiche uguali,
ha una nota, una sola, d'allegrezza:
il mare in fondo alle sue laterali.
Odorata di droghe e di catrame
dai magazzini desolati a fronte,
fa commercio di reti, di cordame
per le navi: un negozio ha per insegna
una bandiera; nell'interno, volte
contro il passante, che raro le degna
d'uno sguardo, coi volti esangui e proni
sui colori di tutte le nazioni,
le lavoranti scontano la pena
della vita: innocenti prigioniere
cuciono tetre le allegre bandiere.

A Trieste ove son tristezze molte,
e bellezze di cielo e di contrada,
c'è un'erta che si chiama Via del Monte.
Incomincia con una sinagoga,
e termina ad un chiostro; a mezza strada
ha una cappella; indi la nera foga
della vita scoprire puoi da un prato,
e il mare con le navi e il promontorio,
e la folla e le tende del mercato.
Pure, a fianco dell'erta, è un camposanto
abbandonato, ove nessun mortorio
entra, non si sotterra piú, per quanto
io mi ricordi: il vecchio cimitero
degli ebrei, cosí caro al mio pensiero,

## Three Streets

There's a street in Trieste
where I go on those days
when misery closes in:
it's called Via del Lazzaretto Vecchio.
The ancient houses all act as my host,
with one sound, one note of welcome:
the sea at the base of their sides.
From the storefronts where no one is shopping
for nets or a rope for his boat,
the odor of drugs and tar;
inside the shop with a flag
for its sign, with their backs
to the self-absorbed world,
workmen serve out their lives;
the colors of nations glimmer
as their faces hover and drain: innocent
convicts threading grief into happy flags.

In Trieste where there's great sadness
and beauty, from above as well as below,
there's a hill called Via del Monte.
It starts with a synagogue
and ends with a cloister,
with a chapel between the two; from a field
above you can make out the black excitement
of life, the sea and the ships and the headland
and the crowds and the draped market stalls.
And next to the hill there's a graveyard
in ruins, which funerals pass
and where no one's been buried for as long
as I can remember: the old cemetery
of the Jews; I think of you constantly,

se vi penso i miei vecchi, dopo tanto
penare e mercatare, là sepolti,
simili tutti d'animo e di volti.

Via del Monte è la via dei santi affetti,
ma la via della gioia e dell'amore
è sempre Via Domenico Rossetti.
Questa verde contrada suburbana,
che perde dí per dí del suo colore,
che è sempre piú città, meno campagna,
serba il fascino ancora dei suoi belli
anni, delle sue prime ville sperse,
dei suoi radi filari d'alberelli.
Chi la passeggia in queste ultime sere
d'estate, quando tutte sono aperte
le finestre, e ciascuna è un belvedere,
dove agucchiando o leggendo si aspetta,
pensa che forse qui la sua diletta
rifiorirebbe all'antico piacere
di vivere, di amare lui, lui solo;
e a piú rosea salute il suo figliolo.

my old ones, whether I mean to or not,
the years of torment and dealing, buried there,
the same soul, and now the same faces.

Via del Monte is a sacred place
but the street for love and excitement
is always Via Domenico Rossetti.
It's just past the center, out where it's green,
but day by day as the trees lose their color
it returns to its place in the city
with an old stateliness intact:
the first few villas,
the first strategic trees.
And for someone who walks there
in the last nights of summer,
where all the windows are open
on the same horizon-filled scene
in which people wait sewing or reading,
it's not uncommon to think, maybe here
delight could reblossom in the pleasure
of being alive, and in loving him, him alone,
and in a fuller life for his son.

## Il garzone con la carriola

È bene ritrovare in noi gli amori
perduti, conciliare in noi l'offesa;
ma se la vita all'interno ti pesa
tu la porti al di fuori.

Spalanchi le finestre o scendi tu
tra la folla: vedrai che basta poco
a rallegrarti: un animale, un gioco,
o, vestito di blu,

un garzone con una carriola,
che a gran voce si tien la strada aperta,
e se appena in discesa trova un'erta
non corre piú, ma vola.

La gente che per via a quell'ora è tanta
non tace, dopo che indietro si tira.
Egli piú grande fa il fracasso e l'ira
piú si dimena e canta.

## The Kid with the Wheelbarrow

It's one thing for us to recharge
our dead love, it helps undo the offenses;
but if it's your own life you feel lacking
why not get out.

Open the window, move around in a crowd: you'll see
                                    how little
contents you: an animal, some game,
or, dressed up in blue,

a kid with a wheelbarrow
whose voice takes up the whole street;
at a drop in a hill
he's no longer running, he flies.

The crowd parts at his calling
and then it moves back.
And the more his commotion, the more people
get mad, the more he bustles and sings.

## L'insonnia in una notte d'estate

Mi sono messo a giacere
sotto le stelle,
una di quelle
notti che fanno dell'insonnia tetra
un religioso piacere.
Il mio guanciale è una pietra.

Siede, a due passi, un cane.
Siede immobile e guarda
sempre un punto, lontano.
Sembra quasi che pensi,
che sia degno di un rito,
che nel suo corpo passino i silenzi
dell'infinito.

Di sotto un cielo cosí turchino,
in una notte cosí stellata,
Giacobbe sognò la scalata
d'angeli di tra il cielo e il suo guanciale,
ch'era una pietra.
In stelle innumerevoli il fanciullo
contava la progenie sua a venire;
in quel paese ove fuggiva l'ire
del piú forte Esaú,
un impero incrollabile nel fiore
della ricchezza per i figli suoi;
e l'incubo del sogno era il Signore
che lottava con lui.

## Insomnia on a Summer Night

I've positioned myself to relax
under the stars,
one of those nights
sick with insomnia,
a religious pleasure.
My pillow is a rock.

A few feet away sits a dog.
He sits immobile and guards
the same distant point.
He's thinking.
He's thinking he's part of a rite.
Through his body
silences pass from the infinite.

Under a sky this blue,
on a night as rich with stars,
Jacob dreamed a ladder of angels
scaling the sky from his pillow
which was a rock.
Beneath countless stars,
the young man counted
his offspring to come;
on the same spot where he'd fled Esau's anger
his more powerful brother,
he imagined an empire
more powerful and crowned
with his own children's riches.
What made him jump from his dream
was the God that fought with him.

## Il canto di un mattino

Da te, cuor mio, l'ultimo canto aspetto,
e mi diletto a pensarlo fra me.

Del mare sulla riva solatia,
non so se in sogno o vegliando, ho veduto,
quasi ancor giovanetto, un marinaio.
La gomena toglieva alla colonna
dell'approdo, e oscillava in mar la conscia
nave, pronta a salpare.
E l'udivo cantare,
per se stesso, ma sí che la città
n'era intenta, ed i colli e la marina,
e sopra tutte le cose il mio cuore:
«Meglio — cantava — dire addio all'amore,
se nell'amore è l'infelicità.»
Lieto appariva il suo bel volto; intorno
era la pace, era il silenzio; alcuno
né vicino scorgevo né lontano;
brillava il sole nel cielo, sul piano
vasto del mare, nel nascente giorno.

Egli è solo, pensavo; or dove mai
vuole approdar la sua piccola barca?
«Cosí, piccina mia, cosí non va»
diceva il canto, il canto che per via
ti segue; alla taverna, come donna
di tutti, l'hai vicino.
Ma in quel chiaro mattino
altro ammoniva quella voce; e questo
lo sai tu, cuore mio, che strane cose
ti chiedevi ascoltando: or se lontana
andrà la nave, or se la pena vana
non fosse, ed una colpa il mio esser mesto.

## The Song of One Morning

I wait for the final song from my heart,
and it delights me to think what it might be.

Along the waterfront in sun,
I don't know if this was a dream, I saw
a sailor, just recently a man.
He unleashed a cable from a landing post
and his boat rocked conscious
ready to sail.
I heard him singing
to himself, so clear
it was as if the city and the seashore
listened, but most of all my heart:
"It's better," he sang, "to forgo a love
if there's misery in loving."
His handsome face appeared content
with that inner silence, that inner peace.
Around me there was no one else;
the sun blazed brilliant in the sky
on a vast and tranquil ocean at the start of day.

He's alone, I thought: now where
does he want to land his boat?
"That way," the song went on, "that way,
my little girl's no good." It was the type
of tune that follows you out doors,
like certain women when you leave a bar.
But that clear morning
it warned of something else,
and my heart knew how to ask
whether the boat had far to go,
whether my life's upset
were a failing or a waste.

Sempre cantando, si affrettava il mozzo
alla partenza; ed io pensavo: È un rozzo
uomo di mare? O è forse un semidio?

Si tacque a un tratto, balzò nella nave;
chiara soave rimembranza in me.

Still singing, the sailor-boy
rushed off; and I thought:
Is he some crude shiphand?
Or a kind of god?

Suddenly the singing stops, he jumps into the boat;
an exquisite image stays with me.

### Dopo la tristezza

Questo pane ha il sapore d'un ricordo,
mangiato in questa povera osteria,
dov'è piú abbandonato e ingombro il porto.

E della birra mi godo l'amaro,
seduto del ritorno a mezza via,
in faccia ai monti annuvolati e al faro.

L'anima mia che una sua pena ha vinta,
con occhi nuovi nell'antica sera
guarda un pilota con la moglie incinta;

e un bastimento, di che il vecchio legno
luccica al sole, e con la ciminiera
lunga quanto i due alberi, è un disegno

fanciullesco, che ho fatto or son vent'anni.
E chi mi avrebbe detto la mia vita
cosí bella, con tanti dolci affanni,

e tanta beatitudine romita!

## After Sadness

This bread has the taste of a memory
swallowed in this sad cafe
by a port even more cluttered and lonely.

I like the bitter taste of the beer
seated outdoors in the middle of the street
where clouded mountains and a lighthouse loom near.

My soul that's just conquered one trouble in life
with new eyes on the ancient night
watches a captain and his pregnant wife

and a ship whose old wooden lines
shine in the sunlight, and a smokestack
the length of two trees, the design's

sophomoric, the kind I made twenty years ago.
And who could have said my life would
be so wonderful, such sweet sorrow

and such secluded bliss!

## Confine

Parla a lungo con me la mia compagna
di cose tristi, gravi, che sul cuore
pesano come una pietra; viluppo
di mali inestricabile, che alcuna
mano, e la mia, non può sciogliere.
                    Un passero
della casa di faccia sulla gronda
posa un attimo, al sol brilla, ritorna
al cielo azzurro che gli è sopra.
                    O lui
tra i beati beato! Ha l'ali, ignora
la mia pena secreta, il mio dolore
d'uomo giunto a un confine: alla certezza
di non poter soccorrere chi s'ama.

## Border Town

She talks a long time, my companion,
about serious, sad things that weigh
the heart down like stone; an inextricable
tangle of hurt that no two
hands can untie.
      A sparrow
stops on the house next door
for a second he shines in the sun,
then he's back in the sky blue above him.
      Oh he
who's blessed among the blessed! With wings
he disregards my secret grief, the pain
a man reaches in a border town,
where he's no help to someone who loves him.

# Tre città

## 1. Milano

Fra le tue pietre e le tue nebbie faccio
villeggiatura. Mi riposo in Piazza
del Duomo. Invece
di stelle
ogni sera si accendono parole.

Nulla riposa della vita come
la vita.

# Three Cities

## 1. Milan

Between your stones and your haze
I spend my vacation. I rest
in the Piazza del Duomo. Instead
of stars
words flicker at night.

Nothing restores life
like living.

## 2. Torino

Ritornerò dentro la cerchia amabile
dei tuoi monti, alle vie che si prolungano
come squilli. Poi tosto in uno strano
silenzio fuggirò ritrovi, amici.
Ma cercherò il soldato Salamano,
il piú duro a parole, il piú al dovere
fermo, che in sé la tua virtú rispecchia.

Cercherò l'officina ov'egli invecchia.

## 2. Turin

I'll come back through the friendly loop
of your mountains, to the streets that stretch
like blaring horns. In the strange
silence that follows I'll escape
to track down my friends.
But the one I'll look for is the soldier Salamano,
the toughest talker, the one with the most
to do, since he reflects all your virtue.

I'll look for him at the office where he grows old.

## 3. Firenze

Per abbracciare il poeta Montale
— generosa è la sua tristezza — sono
nella città che mi fu cara. È come
se ogni pietra che il piede batte fosse
il mio cuore, il mio male
di un tempo. Ma non ho rimpianti. Nasce
— altra costellazione — un'altra età.

### 3. Florence

Out of love for the poet Montale
— his is a generous grief —
I'm in the city I used to love.
It's as if every stone I walk on
were my heart, troubles
of a former time. But I have no regrets. Born now
— in another constellation — another age.

## La gatta

La tua gattina è diventata magra.
Altro male non è il suo che d'amore:
male che alle tue cure la consacra.

Non provi un'accorata tenerezza?
Non la senti vibrare come un cuore
sotto alla tua carezza?
Ai miei occhi è perfetta
come te questa tua selvaggia gatta,
ma come te ragazza
e innamorata, che sempre cercavi,
che senza pace qua e là t'aggiravi,
che tutti dicevano: «E pazza».

È come te ragazza.

## The Cat

Your little cat's gotten skinny.
Its only trouble is love:
trouble your own devotion inspires.

Don't you feel her anxious tenderness?
Don't you hear her purr like a heart
under your hand?
To my eyes she's perfect
like you, your savage cat,
but like you a girl
and a lover who's always hunting,
restlessly roaming here and there,
about whom everyone says, "She's crazy."

She's a girl like you.

## Inverno

È notte, inverno rovinoso. Un poco
sollevi le tendine, e guardi. Vibrano
i tuoi capelli selvaggi, la gioia
ti dilata improvvisa l'occhio nero;
che quello che hai veduto — era un'immagine
della fine del mondo — ti conforta
l'intimo cuore, lo fa caldo e pago.

Un uomo si avventura per un lago
di ghiaccio, sotto una lampada storta.

## Winter

It's night, the ruinous winter. You raise
the blinds a little and look. Your savage
hair shakes in the wind, and pleasure
suddenly dilates your eyes. You've just seen
a glimpse of the end of the world
and it comforts your remote heart,
makes it warm and pleased.

A man sets out on a lake
of ice, under a crooked lamp.

## Finale

L'umana vita è oscura e dolorosa,
e non è ferma in lei nessuna cosa.

Solo il passo del Tempo è sempre uguale.
Amor fa un anno come un giorno breve;
il tedio accoglier numerosi gli anni
può in una sola giornata; ma il passo
suo non sosta, né muta. Era Chiaretta
una fanciulla, ed ora è giovanetta,
sarà donna domani. E si riceve,
queste cose pensando, un colpo in mezzo
del cuore. Appena, a non pensarle, l'arte
mi giova; fare in me di molte e sparse
cose una sola e bella. E d'ogni male
me guarisce un bel verso. Oh quante volte
— e questa ancora — per lui che nessuno
più sa, né intende, sopra l'onte e i danni,

sono partito da Malinconia
e giunto a Beatitudine per via.

## Finale

Life is grim and full of grief,
and nothing about it is certain.

Only the passing of Time is constant.
Love makes a year as short as a day;
boredom can summon ages
to an afternoon; but love's passing
doesn't stop, nor is it quiet. There was Chiaretta
the girl, now in her teens,
tomorrow a woman. For thinking these things
one takes a hit to the middle
of the heart. Art helps keep me
from such thoughts; it turns the fragments
of a life into something singular and beautiful
through me. One good line
restores me. How often
— and this time yet again — for one
neither known nor understood, despite the shame
                                        and trouble

have I set out from Melancholy
and joined Bliss on the way.

Poems 1900 – 1908

## Glauco

Glauco, un fanciullo dalla chioma bionda,
dal bel vestito di marinaretto,
e dall'occhio sereno, con gioconda
voce mi disse, nel natio dialetto:

Umberto, ma perché senza un diletto
tu consumi la vita, e par nasconda
un dolore o un mistero ogni tuo detto?
Perché non vieni con me sulla sponda

del mare, che in sue azzurre onde c'invita?
Qual è il pensiero che non dici, ascoso,
e che da noi, cosí a un tratto, t'invola?

Tu non sai come sia dolce la vita
agli amici che fuggi, e come vola
a me il mio tempo, allegro e immaginoso.

## Glauco

Glauco, boy with the blond mane,
in a sailor's suit
with your steady eyes, and your voice
full of ideas, you'd ask me
through your accent:

Umberto, how come you like to eat
life up but you're never satisfied,
and never let a sorrow
or a secret pass your teeth?
Why won't you come with me

to the beach, whose waves invite
us, surging blue? What's the thought
you won't say that removes you?

You can't imagine how wonderful life feels
for the friends you run off from,
how the time soars, alive and fantastic.

## La casa della mia nutrice

La casa della mia nutrice posa
tacita in faccia alla Cappella antica,
ed al basso riguarda, e par pensosa,
da una collina alle caprette amica.

La città dove nacqui popolosa
scopri da lei per la finestra aprica;
anche hai la vista del mar dilettosa
e di campagne grate alla fatica.

Qui — mi sovviene — nell'età primiera,
del vecchio camposanto fra le croci,
giocavo ignaro sul far della sera.

A Dio innalzavo l'anima serena;
e dalla casa un suon di care voci
mi giungeva, e l'odore della cena.

## The House of My Babysitter

The house of my babysitter
stands silent before an old chapel,
looking down, it almost seems thoughtful
as it tends small goats on a hill.

Through a window she lets in
the city where I was born
with a look at the sorceress sea
and a countryside patterned by work.

There — I remember — my earliest summer
among crosses behind the old church
where I played completely into the night.

To God my soul ascended serene
and from the house the voices I loved
reached me, along with the odor of food.

## A mamma

Mamma, c'è un tedio oggi, una sottile
malinconia, che dalle cose in ogni
vita s'insinua, e fa umili i sogni
dell'uomo che il suo mondo ha nel suo cuore.
Mamma, ritornerà oggi all'amore
tuo, chi un dí l'ebbe a vile?
Chi è solo con il suo solo dolore?

Ed è un giorno di festa, oggi. La via
nera è tutta di gente, ben che il cielo
sia coperto, ed un vento aspro allo stelo
rubi il giovane fiore, e in onde gonfi
le gialle acque del fiume.
Passeggiano i borghesi lungo il fiume
torbido, con violacee ombre di ponti.
Sta la neve sui monti
ceruli ancora; ed il mio cuore, mamma,
strugge, vagante fiamma
nei dí festivi, la malinconia.

E tu pur, mamma, la domenicale
passeggiata riguardi dall'aperta
finestra, nella tua casa deserta
di me, deserta per te d'ogni bene.
Guardi le donne, gli operai (quel bene,
mamma, non scordi) gli operai che i panni
d'ogni giorno, pur tanto utili e belli,
oggi a gara lasciati hanno per quelli
delle feste, sí nuovi in vista e falsi.
Ma tu, mamma, non sai che sono falsi.
Tu non vedi la luce che io vedo.
Altra fede ti regge, che non credo

## For Mother

Mother, there's a tedium today,
some sadness that's got into everything,
even an ambitious man's dreams
show signs of a slow despair.
Mother, try loving
your self-despising son
on a day he's alone
and overcome with grief.

It's a holiday. Crowds
fill up the street
under an overcast
whose wind destroys
the infant flowers
and slaps the river yellow.
Witness the middle class
who can stroll by a turgid river
with its purple mirror bridges.
Snow holds blue to the mountains
while my heart smolders
in an ashy heat.

You, too, mother,
had your careful Sunday walks
to the parlor window
where you'd stare off into space
and dream of the house I deserted,
the one you've scoffed at ever since.
You watch the women
and the workers in the street (they're doing well,
you don't forget), the workers
suited in their Sunday best,

piú, che credevo nella puerizia,
mamma, nella remota puerizia.
Guardi fanciulli con nudi i ginocchi
forti, con nuove in attoniti occhi
voglie, che tra i sudati
giochi nacquero a un tratto in cuore ai piú.
Escono a stormi, vociano, ed il piú
alto con gesta tra di bimbo e d'uomo.
Una giovane passa; ecco, le han dato
del gomito nel gomito.
Irosa ella si volge, e in cor perdona.
Quello addietro rimasto la persona
piega, che un fonte
vide, e di fonte
acqua non costa alla sua sete nulla.

Mamma, non io cosí, mai. La mia culla
io la penso tagliata in strano legno.
Tese l'animo mio sempre ad un segno
cui non tesero i miei dolci compagni.
Mamma, è forse di questo che tu piangi
sempre là nella tua casa deserta?
Lacrimi ancora; e dalla non piú aperta
finestra, con la sera
entra delle campane, entra il profondo
suono, il preludio della dolce notte,
d'un'insonne per te, gelida notte.
Ad ogni tocco piú verso la notte
è roteato il mondo.

Mamma, un tempo ci fu che, le campane
udendo, sulle mie guance una sola
lacrima il vespro amato di viola
tinse, per cose assai dolci e lontane.
Ma quelle guance erano imberbi ancora;

though the clothes left home
are also handsome
and everything hits you as false.
You don't know what false means.
Another faith rules you, the one
I used to believe
in my childhood, mother,
my remote childhood.

Outdoors the boys' naked knees
look amazing. You're struck
by something that you used to want
in the thick of their sweaty play.
They run away shouting,
the tallest among them both baby and man.
A girl goes by
and they give each other the elbow
till she turns on them angry
and forgives in her heart.
The tall one stands near a fountain,
water means nothing to his thirst.

Mother, I was never like that. My cradle
must have been queer. Nothing I want
is like my friends. Is that why
you're still crying in that empty house?
When the night comes in
from the country, the sound
cuts through you. You can't open
a window to that eventual chill.
The second hand pushed at the world.

There was a time, mother,
church bells at morning made me cry
for everything good that's gone away.

ma diverso è il mattino dall'aurora
tanto, che piú me stesso io non conosco.
Quasi un salubre tosco
nel giovane versò la solitaria
forza, onde solo egli è pur fra le genti.
Non vide i passi tuoi farsi piú stanchi,
o dolce madre, e i tuoi capelli bianchi
sulle povere tempie.

Mamma, un tempo fu ancora — il tuo — che in ogni
dottrina la piú saggia eri tenuta
da me, da me che la tua bocca muta
feci poi con l'audacia dei miei sogni.
Tu pel fanciullo eri l'infallibile,
eri colei che non conosce errore.
L'umile tua parola nel suo cuore
si scolpiva cosí ch'ebbe indicibile
angoscia quando, per la prima volta,
pur come ogni altra, la tua mente folta
d'errori, avvolta nel dubbio scoperse.

Mamma, il tempo fu quello che d'avverse
forze piena sentii l'umana vita,
sí che indugio alla mia casa il ritorno.
Ben mi apparvero eterne
verità, ma infinita
n'è l'amarezza, e a sdegno ebbi la grande
casa, il terrazzo ove leggevo Verne,
pallido d'ansia nelle rosse sere.
Poi nel sonno sognavo l'Oriente
barbaro; e quanta gente
non vinceva la mia piccola mano!
Era incerto fra il riso e il pianto il ciglio
tuo su quel sonno; ora è lontano il figlio
unico, e il tempo fugge.

My face was beardless then,
and the mornings now
seem so removed from dawn
I don't know myself.
It's a sweet sort of poison
that isolates a child
from poverty and his mother's fatigue
and blinds him to the whiteness in her hair.

There was a time, mother,
every word you uttered sounded wise.
I listened as if an oracle spoke,
your voice went straight to my dreams.
And that same small heart
burned to discover
you were like all the others, wrong
and secretly unsure.

Those were the years
the pain was too great to go home.
I hated the place, the terrace
where I read Jules Verne
a nervous white in the sunset.
Then I'd dream of his brute Orient
and the numbers that I'd drop
with my little hand!
In my dream
it was never certain
if your smile
was a stage in crying.
Now your only son is far away
and time's flying.

Mamma, il tempo che fugge
t'ansia; e l'ansia che impera
nel tuo cuore c'è, forse, anche nel mio;
c'è, pur latente, il male che ti strugge;
son le tue cure in me domenicali
malinconie.
Lente lente ora sfollano le vie
nella sera di festa, e verdi e rossi
accendono fanali le osterie
di campagna. È una strana sera, mamma,
una che certo affanna
i cuori come il tuo soli ed amanti,
sugli ultimi mari i naviganti,
dentro l'orride celle i prigionieri.
Canterellando scendono i sentieri
del borgo i cittadini,
torna dolce al fanciullo la sua casa;
ed il mistero ond'è la vita invasa
tu con preghiere esprimi.

Mamma, il tempo che fugge
cure con cure alterna; ma in chi sugge
il latte e in chi denuda la mammella
c'è un sangue solo per la vita bella.

Mother, time's flying
makes you afraid, and your fears
are no different than mine,
less latent, maybe,
but the Sunday misery's about the same.
Slowly the crowd returns
the evening to the streets
and lights go on in the country.
It's a strange night, mother,
the kind that makes prisoners
and men at sea worry, hearts
like yours, loving and alone.
When the farmers head out of the city
humming, the house grows sweet again
to your little boy;
and you recognize life's mystery
with your prayers.

Mother, time's flying
turns one problem for the next, but
in the nursing infant and the one who bares her breast
one blood courses and the life is good.

## In cortile

In cortile quei due stavan soletti.
Era l'alba con venti umidi e freschi.
Mi piaceva guardar sui fanciulleschi
volti il cupo turchino dei berretti;

quando l'un l'altro, dopo due sgambetti,
fece presentat'arm colla ramazza.
Seguí una lotta ad una corsa pazza,
colle schiene cozzarono e coi petti.

Mi videro, e Dio sa quale capriccio
sospinse a me quei due giovani cani.
Con molti « Te la sgugni » e « Me la spiccio »,

motteggiando, mi presero le mani.
Ed io sorrisi, ché ai piccoli snelli
corpi, agli atti parevano gemelli.

## In the Courtyard

Two kids were alone in a courtyard.
The wind blew warm at the setting sun.
I was happy to see on those boyish
brows the sober blue of their berets

when one spins round the other
and does a present-arms with a broom.
A fight ensues, then a free-for-all
of colliding chests and backs.

I saw myself, and God knows what mischief
urged me on to those young dogs.
With their constant "Beat its" and "Get losts,"

bickering, they took my hands.
I had to laugh, their light, lanky
bodies, their antics that made them like twins.

## Lettera ad un amico pianista studente al Conservatorio di...

Elio, ricordi il bel tempo gentile,
    l'amicizia fraterna
che ci univa pel gioco nel cortile
    della casa materna?

Eran chiassi, eran salti; un tal nasceva
    suon d'allegria crescente,
che alle finestre intorno si vedeva
    affacciarsi la gente,

fin quando, muto rimprovero, un lume
    nell'interno brillava,
e della sera con le fredde brume
    l'ombra nera calava.

Ma spesso tu sedevi pensieroso
    al cembalo sonoro;
ed io in un canto udivo il dilettoso
    angelico lavoro.

Le tue dita rendevan la canzone
    dell'amor, della vita;
e s'accendeva in me la visione
    d'una pace infinita.

O uno strano presagio il cor m'empiva
    di mestizia profonda.
Ed ecco, sorridendo a noi veniva
    una signora bionda,

## Letter to a Friend Studying Piano at the Conservatory of...

Elio, remember when we were happy,
those times as each other's brother
playing in the yard of your house
that watched over us like a mother?

There'd be screaming and running
till the noise would crescendo
and then we'd notice the folks
appear at the window.

From inside issued the glare
of one reproachful light
as a shadow silently darkened
the mist on the night.

As often you'd be absorbed
at the harpsichord for play.
I'd listen from a corner
to the delightful way

your fingers worked angels
from the keys.
A vision rose in me then
of a personal, infinite peace

at once with an old anxiety,
some sadness clutched at my heart,
and there smiling at the window
a woman made us start,

una bella signora, di cui gli anni
     già volgevano a sera;
     ch'era buona e severa,
che celava ad ognuno i propri affanni,

ch'era tua madre. Elio, è al tuo cor presente
     quella bionda signora?
e nel sonno, o con gli occhi della mente,
     la rivedi tu ancora?

Come tutto mutò! Come la vita
     diversa oggi m'appare!
     Quante immagini care
m'han, via fuggendo, l'alma impaurita!

Quanta dolcezza, quanta ingenua fede
     l'ha in brev'ora lasciata!
Cosí spezzarsi, dileguar si vede
     nube in cielo rosata.

Pace ha tua madre giú nel cimitero.
     Quasi a trarne conforto
a lei va reverente il mio pensiero;
     poi tosto a te lo porto;

a te che sconosciute vie all'intorno
     empiendo vai di suoni;
né, fin che al tutto non è spento il giorno,
     il cembalo abbandoni.

Oh potessi sedermi a te d'accanto!
     Udire quei tranquilli
arpeggi, quelle fughe, quel tuo canto,
     quei tuoi limpidi trilli

a beautiful woman, whose face
showed the network of years
and whose lips drew tight to her mouth
shutting back whatever fears

she felt. She was your mother, Elio.
Do the two of you ever meet
in your sleep, or awake,
do you imagine her figure on the street?

It's so quiet now! Life
seems so difficult these days.
The heart is frightened to witness
one's thoughts run away.

What goodness, what pure faith
in a second gone,
like a cloud one sees vanish
from the sweep of a scarlet dawn.

Peace has your mother in the grave.
It's almost a relief
to watch her moving in my mind
and you in a place that's safe

enough to lose yourself completely
until the day is nearly spent
or to fill up the air with sound
until you quit your instrument.

To sit beside you now would be enough
and listen to those tranquil
tunes, arpeggios and fugues,
your own song's crystal trills

di rosignolo. Io scorderei di certo
     di mia vita l'errore;
ritornerei fanciullo ed inesperto
     dell'umano dolore.

Per te il bel tempo rivivrei gentile,
     l'amicizia fraterna
che ci univa — ricordi? — nel cortile
     della casa materna.

like a nightingale's. I'd be able
to forget my errored life
and return to you a boy
ignorant of human grief.

For you that happiness could be revived,
those times as each other's brother
playing — remember? — in the yard of your house
that watched over us like a mother.

## Ammonizione

Che fai nel ciel sereno
bel nuvolo rosato,
acceso e vagheggiato
dall'aurora del dí?

Cangi tue forme e perdi
quel fuoco veleggiando;
ti spezzi e, dileguando,
ammonisci cosí:

Tu pure, o baldo giovane,
cui suonan liete l'ore,
cui dolci sogni e amore
nascondono l'avel,

scolorerai, chiudendo
le azzurre luci, un giorno;
mai piú vedrai d'intorno
gli amici e il patrio ciel.

## Warning

What are you doing in the sky,
a thunderhead of rose
fondled by light
on the dawn of a cloudless day?

Your shapes shift, and you lose
that sail full of fire
till you break and, disappearing,
warn us that

You, too, young man,
whose hours ring lightly as bells
whose dreams and loves
diminish the grave

will also fade, closing
your own blue eyes one day,
never again to witness
your friends and your father the sky.

## Poems 1935 – 1953

## Il vetro rotto

Tutto si muove contro te. Il maltempo,
le luci che si spengono, la vecchia
casa scossa a una raffica e a te cara
per il male sofferto, le speranze
deluse, qualche bene in lei goduto.
Ti pare il sopravvivere un rifiuto
d'obbedienza alle cose.
                    E nello schianto
del vetro alla finestra è la condanna.

## Broken Glass

Everything's against you. The bad weather,
the lights that blow out, the old
house snapped by a storm and dear to you
for the pain suffered, for the frustrated hopes,
for whatever good you enjoyed.
You think that surviving
disobeys things.
                    In the crash
of the glass is your sentence.

## Amore

Ti dico addio quando ti cerco Amore,
come il mio tempo e questo grigio vuole.
Oh, in te era l'ombra della terra e il sole,
e il cuore d'un fanciullo senza cuore.

**Love**

With you, Love, I give up at the start,
as my grey age would have me do.
Oh, there was the dark of the sun and earth in you,
and the heart of a boy who had no heart.

## Ulisse

Nella mia giovanezza ho navigato
lungo le coste dalmate. Isolotti
a fior d'onda emergevano, ove raro
un uccello sostava intento a prede,
coperti d'alghe, scivolosi, al sole
belli come smeraldi. Quando l'alta
marea e la notte li annullava, vele
sottovento sbandavano piú al largo,
per fuggirne l'insidia. Oggi il mio regno
è quella terra di nessuno. Il porto
accende ad altri i suoi lumi; me al largo
sospinge ancora il non domato spirito,
e della vita il doloroso amore.

## Ulysses

In my youth I sailed
the Dalmatian coast. Rocks
rose up from the surface of waves,
slippery and matted with weeds,
where birds were too intent on their prey
to stop on the emeralds
they became in the sun. When the high
tide and the night submerged them, ships
swerved to the deep, skirting
their snare. Today my kingdom
is no man's land. The port
lights for others its lamps; an unbroken
spirit still calls me to sea,
and a pitiful love for life.

## Il poeta e il conformista

Come t'invidio, amico! Alla tua fede
saldamente ancorato, in pace vivi
con gli uomini e gli dei. Discorri scrivi
agevole, conforme volontà
del tuo padrone. In cambio egli ti dà
pane e, quale sua cosa, ti accarezza.
Arma non ti si appunta contro; spezza
il tuo sorriso ogni minaccia. E passi,
tra gli uomini e gli eventi, quasi illeso.

V'ha chi solo si pensa ed indifeso.
Pensa che la sua carne ha un buon sapore.
Meglio — pensa — chi è in vista al cacciatore
passero che pernice.

## The Poet and the Conformist

How I envy you, friend! You're as certain
as an anchor's fixed,
with men and gods you smoothly mix.
You write with ease, your talk's the same,
all action's in your boss's name.
In exchange for which he throws you bread,
then pets you gently on the head.
He never has to raise a stick,
you smile, and all the world is charmed.

He thinks himself alone, unarmed.
He thinks his flesh is good to chew.
He thinks it better in the hunter's view
to seem the sparrow rather than the hen.

## L'uomo e gli animali

Uomo, la tua sventura è senza fondo.
Sei troppo e troppo poco. Con invidia
(tu pensi invece con disprezzo) guardi
gli animali, che immuni di riguardi
e di pudori, dicono la vita
e le sue leggi. (Ne dicono il fondo).

## Man and Animals

Man, your troubles are an endless pit.
You are too little and you are too much. Envious
(you think it scorn) you stare
at the animals who have no care
nor cause to make them shy, but express
life and know its rules. (They understand the pit.)

## Felicità

La giovanezza cupida di pesi
porge spontanea al carico le spalle.
Non regge. Piange di malinconia.

Vagabondaggio, evasione, poesia,
cari prodigi sul tardi! Sul tardi
l'aria si affina ed i passi si fanno
leggeri.
Oggi è il meglio di ieri,
se non è ancora la felicità.

Assumeremo un giorno la bontà
del suo volto, vedremo alcuno sciogliere
come un fumo il suo inutile dolore.

## Happiness

The young always offer
to shoulder some grief.
They can't take it. They cry with despair.

Vagabond travels, escape, poetry,
precious marvels at night! At night
air refines itself
and sails lightly.
Today is better than yesterday
even if it's still not happiness.

One day we will wear
the pure form of youth, and watch its vain sadness
drift into nothing like smoke.

## Al lettore

Questo libro che a te dava conforto,
buon lettore, è vergogna a chi lo crebbe.
Parlava come un vivo ed era (avrebbe
dovuto, per decenza, essere) morto.

## To the Reader

This book, good Reader, that's made you comforted,
for its writer was a shameful cause.
He spoke like someone living, but he was
(or at least ought to have been) dead.

## Ceneri

Ceneri
di cose morte, di mali perduti,
di contatti ineffabili, di muti
sospiri;

vivide
fiamme da voi m'investono nell'atto
che d'ansia in ansia approssimo alle soglie
del sonno;

e al sonno,
con quei legami appassionati e teneri
ch'ànno il bimbo e la madre, ed a voi ceneri
mi fondo.

L'angoscia
insidia al varco, io la disarmo. Come
un beato la via del paradiso,
salgo una scala, sosto ad una porta
a cui suonavo in altri tempi. Il tempo
ha ceduto di colpo.
                Mi sento,
con i panni e con l'anima di allora,
in una luce di folgore; al cuore
una gioia si abbatte vorticosa
come la fine.
               Ma non grido.
                    Muto
parto dell'ombre per l'immenso impero.

## Ashes

Ashes
of dead things, wasted mistakes,
unspeakable touches, swallowed
sighs;

your vivid
fires finger my pulse
as worry by worry I move
toward the threshold of sleep;

where the same
fierce and gentle embrace
that joins a mother and child
turns me to ashes.

I cross that tortured
passage, and then
like one of the sinless
ascend a flight of stairs
to a door I've known forever
whose time has passed.
                    But for a moment
I'm back in the clothes, back in the spirit
I had then; the light's alive like lightning
until the thrill dissolves, like a heart
come to its end.
                    I do not cry.
                          I make my way mute
from the dark to a giant kingdom.

## Parole

Parole,
dove il cuore dell'uomo si specchiava
— nudo e sorpreso — alle origini; un angolo
cerco nel mondo, l'oasi propizia
a detergere voi con il mio pianto
dalla menzogna che vi acceca. Insieme
delle memorie spaventose il cumulo
si scioglierebbe, come neve al sole.

**Words**


Words,
where all of us first faced
— naked and amazed — our own reflection; I'm looking
for someplace in the world
where the lies that blind you
could be cried away. And together
with that dreadful thinking back
the weight would vanish
as sun undoes the snow.

# Epigrafe

Parlavo vivo a un popolo di morti.
Morto alloro rifiuto e chiedo oblio.

## Epigraph

Alive I spoke to multitudes of dead.
Dead I turn back honors and ask oblivion.